Christmas '98

This gift is to help us
remember our trip to Stone
Mountain and Atlanta, Ga.

love,
Jack

The Scottish Collection

Scottish
RECIPES

HarperCollins*Publishers*

HarperCollins Publishers
PO Box, Glasgow G4 0NB

First published 1998

Reprint 10 9 8 7 6 5 4 3 2 1 0

© HarperCollins Publishers, 1998

ISBN 0 00 472167 5

A catalogue record for this book is available from the British Library

Printed and bound in Italy by Rotolito Lombarda S.p.A., Pioltello

Contents

Scotch Broth

B y virtue of their often damp and chilling climate, the Scots are a nation of enthusiastic soup consumers. While other soups included here are exotically titled, this heroic Scottish soup par excellence has, fittingly, the plainest name of all. Halfway to being a stew, this barley soup is substantial enough to be a meal in itself. Like many soups, its flavours develop well if it is made a day in advance.
Serves 6-8.

2 lb (910 g) neck of mutton or lamb
3 oz (75 g) pearl barley
2 oz (50 g) dried peas, washed and soaked overnight
3–4 carrots, peeled and finely diced
Half a small turnip, peeled and finely diced
3 leeks, well rinsed and chopped
Quarter of a white cabbage, finely chopped
1–2 sticks of celery, chopped
Salt and pepper
3–4 pints (1.7–2.3 litres) of water
Parsley for garnish

- Put the meat in a large pot with the water. Bring to the boil, skim off the scum from the surface, add the barley and peas then simmer gently for about one-and-a-quarter hours.
- Add the chopped vegetables to the pot with the seasoning, bring back to the boil then simmer gently for another hour.
- Remove from the heat and leave aside to cool.
- Lift out the meat, cut it into smaller pieces then return it to the cooling liquid.
- When the soup is quite cold, the fat can easily be removed from the surface.
- Reheat the soup thoroughly, checking the seasoning, and serve it with a sprinkling of chopped parsley.

Cock-a-Leekie

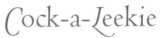

S cots foodies have held a long-running and spirited debate down through the centuries on the merits or otherwise of adding prunes to this dish. Current opinion is definitely in favour, although the plainer and hardier palates of the past pronounced them sweetening to the point of sickliness. The French statesman Talleyrand, a noted gastronome and diplomat, also made the middle-way case for all faint-hearted prune-haters in his pronouncement that they should be included in the cooking, but removed before serving. Another meal in a soup plate, this is both filling and satisfying but relatively low in both calories and with no added fat.
Serves 6–8.

> **One chicken (3–3.5 lb/1.4–1.6 kg); or its equivalent weight in portions with the bones kept in**
> **10 medium-sized leeks, well rinsed and chopped**
> **3 oz (75 g) long-grain rice**
> **18 stoned prunes**
> **2 sprigs of parsley, 2 of thyme and a bay leaf; or 2 stock cubes**
> **Salt and pepper**
> **Water to cover**
> **Parsley for garnish**

- Put the chicken in a large-enough pot, cover with water and bring to the boil. Skim off the scum which rises to the surface.
- Add the herbs, the white parts of the leeks and the seasoning. Return to the boil then turn down to simmer for around two or two-and-a-quarter hours; keeping the heat low will also mean that you do not have to add too much water and so risk diluting the flavours.
- Take the pot off the heat and remove the chicken onto a plate. When it is cool enough to touch, chop up the flesh into small pieces about half the size of a walnut.

- Meanwhile, add the rice and return to a simmer for around 20 minutes. Then return the chicken pieces to the pot together with the prunes and the green parts of the leeks to simmer gently again, for around 20 minutes more.
- Check the seasoning, take out the herbs and serve with a sprinkling of chopped parsley in the centre.

- If you don't have a pot large enough to hold all this, the first part can be done in the oven; simply put the chicken, herbs, white parts of the leeks, seasoning and water into a large casserole and cook at 180 °C, 350 °F, Gas Mark 4 for one-and-a-half hours. Take it out and let it cool down. The skimming of the surface can be done when the cooking liquid has cooled completely. The ingredients will by then be less bulky, allowing you to transfer them to a pot for their final stages.

Partan Bree

*P*artan' is Gaelic for 'crab'; 'bree' means 'soup'. For reluctant or too-imaginative boilers of crustaceans, cooked crabs can be bought from the fishmonger.
Serves 6–8.

> **2 large boiled crabs, or 2 8 oz (225 g) tins of crabmeat**
> **3 oz (75 g) rice**
> **1.5 pints (850 ml) of milk**
> **2 pints (1.15 litres) of chicken stock**
> **5 fl oz (140 ml) of single cream**
> **A dash of anchovy essence**
> **Salt and pepper**
> **Half a teaspoon of grated nutmeg**
> **Parsley for garnish**

- Remove all the meat from the crabs, reserving the meat from the claws.
- Boil the rice in the milk, and when it is cooked liquidise the rice, milk and non-claw meat from the crabs.
- Pour the liquidised soup into a pan with the stock and anchovy essence; add the claw meat and heat through.
- Add the grated nutmeg, check the seasoning and adjust the consistency if necessary, pouring in more water for a runnier soup.
- Stir in the cream just before the soup is served.
- Serve with a sprinkling of chopped parsley in the centre.

Cullen Skink

This oddly named and delicately flavoured soup has its origins in the north-east of Scotland. Finnan haddock is widely regarded as the foremost Scottish smoked fish. If you cannot get it, another smoked haddock can be substituted.
Serves 6.

2 finnan haddock or other smoked haddock
1.5 pints (850 ml) of water
1 pint (600 ml) of milk
2 medium onions, finely chopped
1 oz (25 g) butter
12 oz (340 g) cooked mashed potatoes
Pepper
5 fl oz (140 ml) of single cream
Parsley for garnish

- Put the fish in the water and bring to the boil before turning it down to simmer gently for about 6 minutes, or until the fish is cooked.
- Leave it in the liquid to cool so the smoky flavours of the fish have a chance to infuse.
- Remove the cooled fish from the pan, peel off its skin and bones and flake it with a fork. Leave the flaked meat aside.
- Strain the liquor the fish cooked in, then add the chopped onion to the liquor and simmer for around 15 minutes, or until the onion is cooked.
- Add the milk and butter, then gradually stir in the mashed potatoes to get the soup to the consistency you prefer.
- Grind in some pepper to taste, and liquidise.
- Put the flaked fish back into the soup and reheat.
- Swirl in a little cream and garnish with parsley to serve.

Herrings in Oatmeal
with Sweet Apples

Serves 4.

8 herring fillets
3 tablespoons of medium oatmeal
2 tablespoons of sunflower oil
2 red-skinned eating apples
1 oz (25 g) butter

- Heat the oil in a heavy frying pan. Dip the herring fillets in oatmeal and fry, flesh-side down first, for 3 or 4 minutes on each side or until golden brown.
- Do the fish in 2 or 3 batches and, when one batch is finished cooking, blot it on kitchen paper and keep warm until the others are cooked.
- Then prepare the apples, coring them, but keeping their skins on. Slice them fairly thin.
- Heat the butter in a separate pan and carefully fry the apple slices gently until they are just softening.
- Serve the fish garnished with the apple slices.

Arbroath
Smokie Pâté

*T*hese *delicately flavoured and lightly smoked haddock are among the most popular of Scottish smoked fish. Unlike finnan haddock, they are not split open for smoking, but are tied in pairs at the tail, allowing the flesh in the centre to remain creamy-white.*
Serves 6.

4 smokies
6 oz (175 g) butter, softened
Grated rind of a lemon
Juice of a lemon
Salt and pepper
Parsley to garnish
2 oz (50 g) butter
6 bay leaves

- Flake the flesh out of the smokie skins and beat it, either in a food processor or by hand, together with the softened butter. Then beat in the grated lemon rind and juice and the seasoning.
- Turn the mixture into a loaf tin lined with clingfilm, or individual ramekins. Smooth the surface level and add either sprigs of parsley for garnish or, if you are sealing the pâté with clarified butter, a bay leaf on each portion.
- Chill it in the fridge to firm up.
- Serve with oatcakes, either in the ramekins or turned out of the loaf tin and cut into slices.

Tweed Kettle

*F*ish has always been, and still is, one of the most important foods in the Scots diet, and of all fish salmon is one
of the most highly regarded. But this was not always the case
in the past, when it was more widely available and eaten far
more often than it is now. Such was its plentiful supply that in
the bigger houses it was often fed to the servants – a sure sign
of a lack of regard for the fish. This was a point brought
forcibly home to one particular Scots gentleman travelling in
England with his servant. As he stopped at an inn for the night,
he ordered beef for his own dinner and salmon for his
servant's, only to end up paying more for his servant's meal
than his own. This particular recipe, also known as Salmon
Hash, is a way of poaching a smaller piece of fish rather than
a whole one. It was popular in Edinburgh a century-and-
a-half ago.
Serves 4.

2 lb (910 g) salmon
Salt and pepper
A pinch of ground mace
2 shallots, chopped or 1–2 tablespoons of chives, chopped
6 fl oz (170 ml) of water
3 fl oz (90 ml) of wine vinegar or dry white wine
1 tablespoon of parsley, finely chopped

- Put the fish in a pan together with the water and wine
  vinegar or wine. Bring it to the boil, then turn down
  the heat to simmer for 5 minutes.
- Lift the fish out of the water, peel off the skin, remove
  the bones and cut the meat into one-and-a-half-inch
  cubes.
- Season with salt and pepper, then return it, together
  with the chives or shallot and a sprinkling of mace, to
  the cooking liquor.

- Cover, bring to the boil again then let it simmer gently for a further 25 minutes, or until the fish is tender.
- Stir in the parsley just before serving.

- This dish was traditionally eaten with mushrooms fried in butter, or chopped hard-boiled eggs, and could be served either hot, with mashed potatoes or fresh scones, or cold, with cucumber and cress.

Poached Whole Salmon

*T*his is a special-occasion recipe using salmon as a centre-piece dish. If you do not own a fish kettle, try to hire or borrow one – a good fishmonger will usually lend one to customers.
Serves 16.

A whole 8 lb (3.6 kg) salmon,
cleaned but with head, tail and scales still on
Salt
Fresh dill, parsley and chives
Lemon

❧ Using a measuring jug, pour water into the fish kettle until it comes halfway up the sides. Keep a note of how much water you put in, then add a tablespoon of salt for every 2 pints (1.15 litres) of water you use.

❧ Put the lid on the kettle and bring the water up to the boil.

❧ Remove the lid, carefully place the salmon in and bring the water back to the boil again; then cover it and turn the heat down to simmer gently for 20 minutes.

❧ After that, turn off the heat and leave the salmon in the water until you are ready to serve it. It will retain its heat for up to half an hour.

❧ To serve the salmon, take it out of the water and let it dry off on a rack. Then slip it onto a serving dish to serve it with the skin on or off, with a garnish of herbs such as dill, chives and parsley

❧ Suitable accompaniments for this dish are mayonnaise or a hollandaise sauce.

Loch Fyne
Garlic Mussels

Serves 4.

4 lb (1.8 kg) mussels
6 oz (175 g) butter
6 cloves of garlic, crushed
2 oz (50 g) fresh white breadcrumbs
Juice of a lemon
Parsley, chopped

- If you buy the mussels a day or so in advance, keep them in a large bowl of cold water in the bottom of the fridge.
- When you are ready to prepare them, scrub them thoroughly under cold running water, pulling off any 'beards' (the straggly threads on the long straight side of the shell) and scrape off any barnacles with the back of a knife. Discard any that are already open, or whose shells are cracked or broken.
- Pre-heat the oven to 220 °C, 425 °F, Gas Mark 7; or heat the grill to very hot.
- Put the mussels in a heavy saucepan without adding liquid. Cover and cook on a high heat for a few minutes, shaking the pan from time to time, until the mussels have opened. (Throw away any which haven't.)
- Pull the top shell off each mussel and arrange the half shells containing the mussels in a shallow flameproof dish.
- In another pan, melt the butter then stir in the garlic, breadcrumbs, lemon juice and parsley and scatter this over the mussels.
- Put the dish under the grill or into the oven for about 8 minutes, or until golden brown.

Braised Pheasant
in a Whisky Sauce

*T*he final flavour of this dish depends on the character and flavour of the whisky used.
Serves 3–4.

1–2 pheasant, oven-ready (the bird's weight will depend
on age and gender: a 2 lb or 910 g young hen feeds 2–3 while a
4 lb or 1.8 kg mature cock feeds 4)
2 oz (50 g) butter
1 onion, finely chopped
5 fl oz (140 ml) of malt whisky
5 fl oz (140 ml) of chicken stock
10 juniper berries
Salt and pepper
5 fl oz (140 ml) of double cream
Squeeze of lemon juice

Oven temperature: 190 °C, 375 °F, Gas Mark 5

- Joint the pheasant into breast and leg portions (you can ask your supplier to do this for you). Season these with salt and pepper then, using a casserole which can do double duty for both stove-top and oven, melt the butter and brown the portions on all sides.
- Remove the browned portions and put the chopped onion in to fry, stirring occasionally, until it turns golden brown.
- Meanwhile, warm up half the whisky in a small container left to stand in some very hot water.
- Replace the pheasant portions in the pan, pour over the warmed whisky and, standing at arm's length, set it alight.

- When the flames die down, add the juniper berries, seasoning and chicken stock. Let it warm through on the cooker top, then cover it and place it in the pre-heated oven.
- Cook it for 45–60 minutes or until tender – an older bird will take longer.
- Remove the cooked pheasant portions to a pre-heated serving dish to finish the sauce.
- Strain the sauce then boil it down until it thickens.
- Stir in the other half of the whisky, the cream and the lemon juice, and heat it through without boiling.
- Serve the sauce over or beside the pheasant.

Traditional Cattle-Raider's Grace

He that ordained us to be born,
Send us mair meat for the morn,
Come by right or come by wrang,
Christ, let us not fast ower lang,
But blithely spend whea't blithely got.
Ride, Rowland, hough's i' th' pot!

Festive Pheasant

Serves 3–4.

1–2 pheasant, oven-ready (the bird's weight will depend
on age and gender: a 2 lb or 910 g young hen feeds 2–3 while a
4 lb or 1.8 kg mature cock feeds 4)
Salt and pepper
1 oz (25 g) butter
1 tablespoon of olive oil
8 oz (225 g) pickling onions, peeled
8 oz (225 g) canned whole chestnuts
2 tablespoons of flour
7 fl oz (200 ml) of dry white wine
5 fl oz (140 ml) of chicken stock
1 tablespoon of redcurrant jelly
Rind of an orange, cut in julienne strips *
Juice of 2 oranges
2 tablespoons of brandy
1 bay leaf

* Peel the orange skin with a potato peeler, which should let you
avoid the bitter white pith. Then cut these strips into matchstick-
like strips with a sharp knife.

Oven temperature: 180 °C, 350 °F, Gas Mark 4

- ⊗ Joint the pheasant into breast and leg portions, season
  these with salt and pepper then melt the butter and oil
  in a pan to brown the portions on all sides.
- ⊗ Transfer these to a casserole, then fry the onions in the
  same pan for about 5 minutes or until they have begun
  to change colour.

- Gradually at first, and still stirring, pour in the stock and the wine; bring everything up to the boil.
- Stir in the redcurrant jelly, orange rind and juice, brandy and bay leaf.
- Season and pour carefully over the pheasant.
- Cover the casserole and cook for 60 minutes or until the pheasant is tender.
- Serve with some of the sauce with the julienne strips over the pheasant.

Roast Venison

Serves 6–8.

Marinade
1.25 pints (750 ml) of red wine
5 fl oz (140 ml) of red wine vinegar
5 fl oz (140 ml) of olive oil
Juice of a lemon
1 onion, sliced
1 carrot, sliced
2 cloves of garlic, crushed
8 peppercorns
4 cloves
Sprig of thyme and marjoram
1 bay leaf
Meat
4 lb (1.8 kg) haunch of venison
4 oz (100 g) butter

Oven temperature: 230 °C, 450 °F, Gas Mark 8

- *Marinade:* Put all the ingredients into a large pan, bring it to the boil and simmer for 5 minutes. Let it cool down and transfer it to a large bowl. Put in the meat and leave it there for at least 2 days, turning and basting it every 8 hours.
- *Meat:* Take the meat out and pat it dry with kitchen paper, then strain the marinade and measure out 15 fl oz (425 ml) of it. Rub the butter all over the venison, then set it in a roasting pan with the 15 fl oz of marinade. Roast it in the preheated oven: 15 minutes to the pound and 15 over for very rare meat, 20 minutes per pound and 20 over for medium-rare, and 25 per pound and 25 over for medium–well-done. Baste it regularly with the roasting pan juices. Let the cooked meat rest for 10 minutes before serving with a rowan or red-currant jelly, or the boiled-down roasting-pan juices.

Venison Collops
with a Fruity Claret Sauce

Serves 4.

Collops
4 venison steaks, each weighing about 6–7 oz (175–200 g)
Salt and pepper
4 tablespoons of sunflower oil

Sauce
3 tablespoons of cranberry jelly
Grated rind and juice of half an orange
Grated rind and juice of half a lemon
4 fl oz (110 ml) of claret
Salt and pepper
Pinch of cayenne pepper

- *The Sauce:* Make the sauce as far ahead of cooking as possible – half a day is good, a few days is better. Put all the ingredients except the claret into a pot and, stirring well, bring them to simmering point. Then take them off the heat, pour in the claret, stir and keep aside until you cook the dish.

- *The Collops:* Season the steaks well while the oil is heating. When the oil is smoking hot, quickly lay the steaks in; cook for four-and-a-half to five minutes on each side for half-inch-thick steaks to be done medium-rare.

- *The Dish:* Keeping the pan on the heat, remove the steaks to warmed serving plates and quickly pour the sauce into the pan. Keep the heat up so that it boils and bubbles for a minute or two, and stir it occasionally to get any residues up from the pan. When it is thickened, pour it over the steaks to serve.

Ayrshire Chicken and Leek Pie

Serves 6–8.

Pastry
8 oz (225 g) flour
A pinch of salt
4 oz (100 g) butter
3–4 tablespoons of cold water
Filling
2 lb (910 g) leeks, washed and chopped
1 onion, sliced
3–3.5 lb (1.35–1.6 kg) chicken
1 lb (450 g) boiling ham
1 teaspoon of dried thyme, or 1 tablespoon of fresh
Half a teaspoon of grated nutmeg
Salt and pepper
4 fl oz (110 ml) of whipping or double cream

Oven temperature: 200 °C, 400 °F, Gas Mark 6

- *The Filling:* Put the leeks, onion, chicken, ham, thyme, nutmeg, salt and pepper in a large pot and cover everything with water. Bring it to a boil then turn it down, cover and let it simmer for one-and-a-half hours or until the chicken is tender. When it is cooked, turn off the heat and leave it to stand for an hour. Meanwhile, make the pastry.
- *The Pastry:* Sift the flour and salt together, then rub in the butter until the mixture resembles breadcrumbs. Sprinkle just as much water over it as is needed to bring it together into a dough that comes away cleanly from the sides of the bowl. Wrap it in clingfilm and leave it to rest in the fridge for 30 minutes.

Assembling the Pie:

Fish out the chicken and the ham and cut the meat up into fairly thick slices. Using a slotted spoon, remove the leeks and onion to a plate. Reserve the stock from the pot. Layer the chicken, ham and vegetables in a 3 pint (1.7 litre), deep pie dish, repeating the 3 layers as you go. Pour in the cream, then the stock to bring the level of the liquid up to within half an inch of the top.

Roll out the prepared pastry larger than the size of the pie dish. Wet the rim of the dish with some of the left-over stock, then lay the pastry down on top; press down at the edges, finishing them off by pinching them between fingers and thumb, crimping as you go round. Cut off the extra pastry which can be shaped and used for decorating the pie, and pierce 2 holes in the centre. Brush the pastry with milk.

Bake for 15 minutes, then turn down the heat to 180 °C, 350 °F, Gas Mark 4 and bake for 15 minutes more or until the crust is a golden-brown colour.

Scots Steak Pie

*A*lways more popular in Scotland than its variant with kidney, this pie has been a victim of its own popularity and has suffered at the hands of some careless mass caterers. Its home-made version, however, remains superb.

Serves 4–6.

Pastry
12 oz (350 g) prepared puff pastry
Filling
2 lb (910 g) rump steak
2 tablespoons of flour
3 tablespoons of olive oil
1 onion, finely chopped
10 fl oz (280 ml) of beef stock
1 teaspoon of Worcester sauce
1 teaspoon of chopped parsley
Salt and pepper

- Cut the steak into cubes of about half or three-quarters of an inch. Season the flour with salt and pepper and roll the steak cubes about in it until they are well coated.
- Using a large pan, heat the oil and brown the steak cubes in it, frying them in batches; keep them warm.
- Fry the onion in the remaining oil for about 5 minutes or until it becomes translucent.
- Then put the meat back in, sprinkle over any remaining seasoned flour and add the beef stock, Worcester sauce and parsley; stir well to get all the residues up from the bottom.
- Bring it all to the boil and spoon off any scum which rises to the surface.
- Cover the pan and let it simmer for about an hour or until the meat is tender.

- ⊲ Check the seasoning and stir it occasionally but carefully to avoid breaking the steak chunks. Let it cool.
- ⊲ To bake the pie, preheat the oven to 220 °C, 425 °F, Gas Mark 7.
- ⊲ Put the meat into a 2 pint (1.2 litres) pie dish.
- ⊲ Unless you are unpressurised enough to enjoy the challenge of pastry-making, buy some frozen puff pastry.
- ⊲ Roll it out on a lightly floured board to a depth of about half an inch, moisten the rim of the pie dish and lay the pastry onto it.
- ⊲ Press the edges firmly to seal it, then finish them by decorating with a fork pattern, or pinching them between your fingers as you wish.
- ⊲ Decorate the top with some pastry leaves, cut 2 vents in the centre of the pie, and brush the surface with milk or beaten egg.
- ⊲ Bake for 20 minutes, then turn the heat down to 190 °C, 375 °F, Gas Mark 5, and bake for another 15–20 minutes, or until the pastry is crisp and golden.

Pan-Fried
Scotch Steaks

*T*his recipe uses two of Scotland's finest products – Aberdeen Angus beef and whisky. The quality of the ingredients is important, as is the timing – be careful not to overcook the meat.
Serves 4.

4 8–10 oz (225–275 g) Aberdeen Angus sirloin steaks; remove from the fridge at least 2 hours before cooking
Salt and pepper
1 oz (25 g) butter
1 dessertspoon of sunflower oil
2 fl oz (50 ml) of whisky
10 fl oz (280 ml) of double cream

- Warm the serving plates. Put the oil and butter in a heavy frying pan, stirring together as the butter melts, until it is very hot and the butter is foaming.
- Then place in the seasoned steaks, one at a time.
- Lower the heat to medium and cook, turning the steaks once only during the cooking time: 3–4 minutes for rare steaks, 4–5 for medium and 5–6 for well done. The exact time will depend on the thickness of the steak, but if it feels soft in the middle when you press it with the back of a fork, the meat should still be rare; firmness indicates that it is well done. Take the meat out to the warmed serving plates.
- With the heat high again, pour the whisky into the pan and scrape up all the sediment from the base; let it boil to reduce it a bit, then turn the heat right down to add the cream.
- Simmer for a few minutes over a low heat so that the cream thickens and mixes with the other flavours.
- Season to taste and serve over or around the steaks.

Forfar Bridies

A pasty-type preparation.
Makes 5 or 6 bridies.

Pastry
1 lb (450 g) flour
8 oz (225 g) lard
A good pinch of salt
Cold water to mix
Milk to glaze
Filling
1 lb (450 g) rump steak
2 small onions, finely chopped
2 oz (50 g) suet or butter

Oven temperature: 220 °C, 425 °F, Gas Mark 7

- Sift the flour and the salt, then rub in the lard.
- Add water to make a stiff dough. Wrap it in clingfilm and leave to rest in the fridge for 30 minutes.
- Bat out the meat flat with a meat bat or rolling pin. Cut it into thin strips, then bat it again. Cut it across the strips now into small lengths of a half to one inch.
- Mix this with the onion, suet or butter and seasoning.
- When the dough has rested, divide it into 5 or 6 portions and, on a lightly floured board, roll these out into ovals.
- Spoon the filling down one half of each pastry oval, moisten the edges and fold the other half over.
- Squeeze the edges together, crimping them with fingers and thumb to seal. Make 2 small slits in the top of each before brushing with a little milk.
- Bake on a greased baking tray for about 20 minutes, or until the pastry starts to look brown.
- Turn the heat down to 190 °C, 375 °F, Gas Mark 5, and bake for 30 minutes more, or until the meat is cooked.

Haggis
and Trimmings

A word about Scottish soul food . . .

*D*espite its place as a high-kitsch national icon, haggis really is eaten enthusiastically in Scotland. Its combination of traditional ingredients, peppery–spicy taste, comforting texture and endless adaptability is an irresistible one that has pleased palates as diverse as labourers, poets, royals and foodies.

But to the ambitious who feel they could have a go at making this most Scottish of dishes, a bit of advice – don't try it. Haggis-making involves doing fairly disgusting things with the windpipe, stomach bag and other assorted innards of a sheep, and by the time you are finished, eating it may well be the last thing on your mind. With so many superb-quality commercially prepared haggises available, only the fanatically tradition-obsessed would bother to cook their own.

Instead, concentrate your skills on making the traditional trimmings to go with your bought haggis – either mashed neeps and potatoes served separately, or in Clapshot (see opposite).

A 2 lb (910 g) haggis will serve 4–6 as a main course, depending on appetites.

Clapshot

The traditional accompaniment for haggis.
Serves 4.

1 lb (450 g) potatoes, preferably a dry and floury variety, peeled
1 lb (450 g) turnip, peeled and diced
2 oz (50 g) butter
1 tablespoon of chives, finely chopped
Salt and white pepper

- Using separate pots, boil the potatoes and the turnips for about 20 minutes, or until they are soft.
- Drain, and return them to their cooking pots to dry out a little, stirring to make sure they don't stick.
- Mash them together thoroughly, then turn back into one of the pots again to re-heat carefully.
- Add the butter, chives and seasoning, fluff up with a fork and serve hot.

Potato Scones

Mostly eaten at teatime as a snack, or fried with bacon at breakfast, much in the American style of hash-browns, versatile potato scones could be made much more use of in pancake or stuffed-pasta dishes, and are an ideal re-hash of extra mash.

Makes about 20.

8 oz (225 g) mashed potatoes,
preferably a dry and floury variety, slightly heated
1 oz (25 g) butter, melted
A good pinch of salt
2–3 oz (50–75 g) plain flour

⊗ Mix the butter and salt into the mashed potatoes, then gradually add in as much flour as the potatoes can take without becoming too dry.

⊗ Separate the dough into 5 pieces and on a lightly floured board roll each piece out into an 8 inch (20 cm) round; cut into quarters.

⊗ Prick with a fork and cook on a lightly greased hot griddle or non-stick pan, turning as each side begins to brown (about 3 minutes).

⊗ Keep warm while the other batches are made.

Stovies

Serves 4–6.

1 lb (450 g) onions, thinly sliced
2 oz (50 g) butter
2 lb (910 g) potatoes, thinly sliced
Salt and pepper
3–6 tablespoons of stock
Chives or parsley, chopped

- Melt the butter in a pan and fry the onions at a low heat until they are soft.
- As they cook, slice the potatoes to about quarter-inch thickness, then add these to the pan, stirring well to coat them with the butter.
- Add the seasoning, cover the pan and leave on a low heat for about 10 minutes, checking once or twice to ensure the potatoes do not stick.
- Then add the stock – about 3 tablespoons for drier stovies, about 6 tablespoons for more moist ones.
- Cover again and this time cook until the potatoes are soft.
- At this point, before serving, other cooked meats can be added to the dish and stirred through.
- The stovies can be browned by increasing the heat for a few minutes before serving, then stirring.
- Serve with a sprinkling of chives or parsley.

Mushroom and Garlic Cups

Makes 4 cups.

Cups
6 sheets of ready-made filo pastry
2 oz (50 g) butter, melted
Filling
0.5 oz (20 g) butter
2 cloves of garlic, crushed
1 lb (450 g) mushrooms, wiped or brushed but not washed
1 tablespoon of chives
2 teaspoons of Dijon mustard
1 tablespoon of lemon juice

Oven temperature: 180 °C, 350 °F, Gas Mark 4

✎ ***The Cups:*** Lay a sheet of filo on a board and brush it
with butter. Lay down the next on top of it, brush again
and repeat the process until all the sheets are used up.
Then cut the pastry into quarters and, to shape the
quarters into cups, press each into a ramekin lined with
baking parchment which comes up over the top of the
ramekin (this will make it easier to remove the pastry
when it is cooked). Bake in the pre-heated oven for
10minutes or until golden in colour, then remove from
the ramekins to serving plates. While the cups are
baking, make the filling.

✎ ***The Filling:*** Over a moderate heat, melt the butter in a
heavy frying pan and add the garlic; fry for half a
minute, stirring so it does not stick. Then add the
mushrooms, chives, mustard and lemon juice; cover
the pan and cook for 4–5 minutes or until the
mushrooms are soft. Spoon the filling into the cups
and serve immediately.

Lanark Blue Cheesecake

A savoury cheesecake made with one of the great Scottish cheeses.

Serves 6–8.

Base
8 oz (225 g) wholemeal bran biscuits, crushed
3 oz (75 g) butter, melted

Filling
3 large eggs
8 oz (225 g) curd cheese
6 oz (170 g) Lanark Blue
3 fl oz (85 ml) of single cream
1 oz (25 g) chives, chopped
Salt and pepper

Oven temperature: 190 °C, 375 °F, Gas Mark 5

- Crumb the biscuits in a food processor.
- Stir in the melted butter, then press the mixture into an 8 inch (20 cm) flan dish or tin. Leave to set in the fridge.
- Meanwhile, blend the eggs, curd cheese, cream and seasoning.
- Crumble the Lanark Blue into small pieces and mix in together with the chives.
- Spread this mixture on top of the biscuit base and bake in the pre-heated oven for 35–40 minutes or until springy in the centre.

Cheese and Egg Pie

*T*his is not really a pie, but a modified version of a dish known by that name to generations of Scottish school-children. This recipe uses hard-boiled eggs instead of the more normal scrambled ones.

Serves 4.

8 eggs, hard-boiled
1 oz (25 g) butter
1 oz (25 g) flour
1 pint (600 ml) of milk
1 teaspoon of Dijon mustard
6 oz (175 g) strong Cheddar cheese, grated
Salt and pepper
A pinch of cayenne pepper
4 tablespoons of freshly grated Parmesan

Oven temperature: 180 °C, 350 °F, Gas Mark 4

- Shell the eggs, slice them and layer them in the bottom of a shallow, pre-greased oven-proof dish.
- Melt the butter in a pan then stir in the flour and cook for 1–2 minutes, stirring all the time.
- Then add the milk a little at a time, stirring between each addition to get the lumps out.
- When all the milk has been added, let the sauce bubble, continuing to stir it vigorously.
- Stir in the mustard, then turn down the heat and stir in all the grated cheese.
- Do not allow it to boil at this stage, or it will become stringy.
- Season and add a small pinch of cayenne.
- Pour the cheese sauce over the eggs, season the top and sprinkle a grating of Parmesan on top.
- Bake in the pre-heated oven for 15 minutes, or until the sauce is bubbling gently.

Whipped Syllabub

T his sweet cream dish is ideal with fresh soft fruit or shortbread fingers.
Serves 6.

4 fl oz (110 ml) of white wine
2 fl oz (60 ml) of brandy
Grated rind and juice of 2 small lemons
4 oz (100 g) caster sugar
Quarter-teaspoon of ground cinnamon
1 pint (600 ml) of double cream

- Mix together the wine, brandy, lemon juice and rind, sugar and cinnamon in a pan.
- Let it simmer for a few minutes to bring out the flavours, then leave the pan, covered, for a few hours or overnight.
- Strain the liquid and pour it into wine glasses.
- Whip the cream until it is stiff, then spoon the cream in on top of the liquid. It can be decorated with a few shavings of lemon zest
- If the syllabub is served with fruit, the liquid and cream can be mixed together to make it an all-in-one floppy, flavoured cream.

Cranachan

Its place as a sweet dish dictates that cranachan should be listed as a pudding, but its main ingredient qualifies its inclusion here.

Serves 4.

> 1 pint (600 ml) of double cream
> 2 oz (50 g) pinhead oatmeal
> 4 tablespoons of heather honey
> 4 tablespoons of whisky or Stag's Breath Liqueur
> 8 oz (225 g) raspberries

- Toast the oatmeal, either in the oven, under the grill or in a pan on the stove-top, until it is dried out but not browned; this concentrates its nutty flavours. Leave it aside to cool.
- Whip the cream until it is frothy, but not stiff, stirring in the whisky or liqueur as you go.
- Then stir in the honey, checking it for sweetness before you add it all, and the oatmeal.
- Mix in the raspberries, reserving some of these to decorate the top of the serving dishes.
- Spoon the cream mixture into glasses, topping with the remaining raspberries.

Oaty
Rhubarb Crumble

Serves 4–6.

2 lb (910 g) rhubarb, cut into 1 inch bits
6 oz (150 g) white sugar
Grated rind of an orange
5 oz (125 g) flour
3 oz (75 g) pinhead oatmeal
3 oz (75 g) butter

Oven temperature: 200 °C, 400 °F, Gas Mark 6

- Put the rhubarb chunks into a pie dish and sprinkle over 3 oz (75 g) of the sugar and half the orange rind.
- Rub the butter into the flour until the mixture looks like breadcrumbs, then stir in the oatmeal and the rest of the sugar and orange rind.
- Spoon this crumble mixture over the rhubarb, pressing it down very lightly.
- Bake in the pre-heated oven for about 50 minutes.
- Serve warm with a good custard, or cream.

Spicy
Fruity Puddings

T his is a baked version of a traditional steamed pudding, lightened by breadcrumbs instead of flour. Serve it with a traditional Scottish pudding accompaniment, Wine Sauce (see opposite).

Makes 6 puddings.

4 oz (100 g) white breadcrumbs
Half a teaspoon of baking powder
A large pinch of ground cinnamon
A large pinch of grated nutmeg
A large pinch of ground cloves
2 oz (50 g) caster sugar
4 oz (100 g) sultanas (or a mix of other dried fruit)
3 oz (75 g) butter, softened, or shredded suet
1 egg, beaten
3 fl oz (90 ml) of milk

Oven temperature: 180 °C, 350 °F, Gas Mark 4

- Pre-grease six dariole moulds for individual puddings.
- Mix together all the dry ingredients and the butter.
- Make a well in the middle, add the egg and draw the mixture together.
- Then add the milk, a little at a time, to bring the mixture to a soft, dropping consistency.
- Spoon it into the dariole moulds, cover them with foil and bake them for 45 minutes.
- Turn them out onto individual serving plates and serve the sauce separately.

Wine Sauce

Grated rind of a lemon
3 fl oz (85 ml) of water
2 oz (50 g) caster sugar
1 oz (25 g) butter
1 teaspoon of flour
8 fl oz (225 ml) of sweet white wine or sweet sherry
Juice of a lemon

- Put the grated lemon rind, water and sugar in a pan and bring it up to the boil; let it simmer for 10 minutes.
- Work the butter and flour together and stir them in 2 or 3 batches, into the cooked syrup in the pan.
- Finally, pour in the sweet wine and lemon juice and bring it up to the boil, stirring continuously, for a minute.
- Pour the sauce around the puddings, or serve separately.

Lemon Tart

*T*he use of ground almonds in the lemon filling gives this tart a lighter texture and flavour than some other more traditional recipes.

Serves 6.

Tart
5 oz (140 g) plain flour
2 tablespoons of caster sugar
4 oz (100 g) butter
1 egg yolk
Filling
3 egg whites
3 oz (75 g) butter
3 oz (75 g) caster sugar
4 oz (100 g) ground almonds
2 egg yolks
Grated rind and juice of 1 lemon
Icing sugar, to dust

Oven temperature: 190 °C, 375 °F, Gas Mark 5

- Sift the flour, add the sugar and rub in the butter until the mixture looks like breadcrumbs.
- Drop in the egg yolk and cut and stir it in, drawing the mixture together into a dough.
- Cover it with clingfilm and put it in the fridge to rest for 30 minutes.
- Press the rested dough into an 8 inch (20 cm) loose-bottomed flan tin, prick it several times and bake it blind in the pre-heated oven for 10 minutes.
- Remove it from the oven, take away the lining paper and weights, and brush the pastry case with a little lightly beaten egg white which will be used for the filling; then return it to the oven and leave it for another 10 minutes.

- Remove it, and turn down the oven to 160 °C, 325 °F, Gas Mark 3.
- For the filling, whisk up the egg whites to stiff peaks; set aside.
- Beat the butter and sugar together until they are light and fluffy, then fold in the almonds and the egg yolks.
- Combine the lemon juice and rind and mix these in, then carefully fold in the whisked egg whites.
- Spoon the filling into the pastry case, smooth down the top with the back of a spoon and bake for 15–20 minutes, or until a skewer inserted into the centre comes out clean.
- Take the tart from the oven and let it cool slightly before dusting the top with icing sugar.
- Serve warm or cold, with cream.

Scones

S cotland has many different types of scones, both sweet and savoury. The following is the basic recipe for milk scones.
Makes 8.

8 oz (225 g) plain flour
3 teaspoons of baking powder
2 oz (50 g) butter
A pinch of salt
5 fl oz (140 ml) of milk

Oven temperature: 230 °C, 450 °F, Gas Mark 8

- Grease the griddle and pre-heat it until moderately hot.
- Sift the dry ingredients into a bowl together, then rub in the butter.
- Make a well in the middle and pour in the milk; mix until it comes together in a soft, pliable dough.
- Turn out onto a lightly floured surface and knead very lightly until smooth.
- Roll or press the dough out to a half-inch thickness, cut it into rounds, or leave as one large scone-cake, and dust with flour, or brush with milk or beaten egg.
- Cook on the griddle or bake in the pre-heated oven for around 12 minutes.

The following flavours are easy variations on the basic milk scone recipe.

Rich Sweet Scones: Substitute cream for the milk (it can be sour cream) and add a beaten egg.
Fruit Scones: Add 2–3 oz (50–75 g) sultanas.
Raspberry Scones: Add 3–4 oz (75–100 g) raspberries and a tablespoon of sugar.
Herb Scones: Add 1 scant teaspoon of dried herbs, or 2–3 teaspoons of fresh.
Cheese Scones: Add 4 oz (100 g) grated cheddar.

The Scots Cook

A noted Scots cookery writer has said, 'If every Frenchwoman is born with a wooden spoon in her hand, every Scotswoman is born with a rolling-pin under her arm.' Although the different lifestyles and pressures of the modern world have seen off these traditional baking skills in most homes, Scotland does still retain a wonderful legacy of baking recipes.

Soda Scones

*A*s with Irish soda bread, bicarbonate of soda was the traditional leavening agent for these scones – hence the name.

Makes 4 scones.

8 oz (225 g) plain flour
3 teaspoons of baking powder
Quarter-teaspoon of salt
4–5 fl oz (110–140 ml) of milk

For oven-baked scones, pre-heat the oven to 220 °C, 425 °F, Gas Mark 7. For griddle-cooked scones, pre-heat the griddle as you begin.

- Sift the dry ingredients together into a bowl, and mix them well.
- Add the milk gradually and mix to a soft dough; if the mixture seems too dry, add a little more at a time.
- Divide into 4 equal pieces and roll them into half-inch-thick rounds. These can be marked off into quarters.
- Dust with flour and bake on a hot, lightly floured griddle until they are cooked all the way through – 8–10 minutes on the first side, 5–6 on the second.
- For oven baking, place the rounds on a lightly floured baking tray for 10–15 minutes.
- Soda scones are split and eaten with butter, jam or honey.

Pancakes

Scotch pancakes – also known as Drop Scones – are quite different from 'normal' pancakes. They are thick, sweet and cakey in consistency, only around 3 inches wide but up to half an inch thick.

1 lb (450 g) plain flour
1 oz (25 g) baking powder
3 oz (75 g) sugar
Half a teaspoon of salt
2 tablespoons of syrup
2 eggs
Approx. 10 fl oz (280 ml) of milk

- Lightly grease and pre-heat a griddle or heavy non-stick frying pan to fairly hot.
- Sift the dry ingredients into a bowl.
- Mix the syrup, eggs and milk together then add these to the dry ingredients; beat them together until the batter is smooth. The consistency should be thick but runny.
- Drop the mixture, a tablespoon at a time, onto the griddle or pan. They should spread up to about 3 inches (7 cm) and maintain some thickness.
- Watch the pancakes for the upper surface beginning to bubble – this should indicate that the underside is ready to turn: it should be lightly browned.
- Up to two minutes on either side should be enough to cook them.
- Keep the cooked pancakes warm until all batches are cooked.
- Scotch pancakes are eaten with butter and the usual sweet preserves.

Shortbread

*U*nlike porridge, which is surrounded by so much tartan-kitsch mythology, shortbread is a 'Scottish' food that is really and truly eaten by most Scots. Although highly regarded all year round, its sales shoot up at the festive period, a fact in keeping with its history, which has always been associated with celebration: in the days when it was made primarily with oatmeal, it was the wedding cake of Scotland and was known as Bride's Cake. Tradition had it that the cake should be crumbled over the new bride's head, confetti-like, as she entered her new home after the wedding. If the cake broke into crumbs, it was a good omen of a fruitful marriage; lumpy cake, however, was taken to indicate possible infertility. The young women in the wedding party would take portions of the scattered crumbs home to help them dream of their future husband.

   There are only three basic ingredients in shortbread and, as ever in such a basic food, the best results are achieved by using the finest ingredients: soft, white flour, good-quality butter for the shortening and the main flavouring, and fine caster sugar. Of course, variations are always possible and ways of re-inventing a classic recipe in a new way are always welcomed.

12 oz (350 g) plain flour (4 oz, or 100 g, of this can be rice flour or semolina)
8 oz (225 g) butter, softened
4 oz (100 g) sugar
A pinch of salt

Oven temperature: 150 °C, 300 °F, Gas Mark 2

- Cream the butter and sugar together.
- Sift the flour and salt together, then bring them gradually into the creamed mixture until it looks like a shortcrust mix.
- Do not knead or roll the mixture, but pat and press it into 2 8 inch (20 cm) rounds, using a variety of

methods: a lightly buttered, fluted, loose-bottomed flan tin on a baking tray; a lightly buttered and floured wooden shortbread mould, levelled off and knocked out onto a baking paper-lined baking tray; or your hand. In any case, the shortbread's thickness should be around three-quarters of an inch.

- Pinch the edges all the way round with your finger and thumb to give the characteristic lightly crimped appearance, and prick all over with a fork.
- Bake in the pre-heated oven for about 60–70 minutes or until the shortbread is a pale-gold biscuity colour.
- Remove and mark the surface into portions, whether wedges or one-and-a-half-inch-thick fingers for a square-baked shortbread; dust with caster sugar immediately.
- If you have baked the shortbread in a tin, leave it to cool there.

Millionaire's Shortbread, or Caramel Shortcake

A few additions to the basic shortbread recipe gives this very sweet and sticky soft-toffee biscuit, a popular teatime treat.

- Make the shortbread in a square or rectangular tin, but to a thickness of about quarter of an inch.
- Make the caramel by boiling an unopened tin of condensed milk in a pot of water for 3 hours; make sure the tin is always covered with boiling water, and keep topping the level up as necessary.
- Let it cool, open it and spread it over the shortbread to a depth of about half an inch.
- Then, break up a few ounces of chocolate cake-covering or chocolate (white, milk or plain according to your preference), heat to melt and pour it over; the chocolate topping should be a wafer-thin film on top, of about an eighth of an inch.
- Let it cool and cut it into two-and-a-half-inch squares.

Cloutie Dumpling

The name of this pudding comes from 'clout', the old Scots name for a cloth, in which the pudding is boiled. Makers of traditional Christmas puddings will recognise the method of preparation and cooking.

8 oz (225 g) plain flour
1 rounded teaspoon of baking powder
4 oz (100 g) oatmeal
4 oz (100 g) suet or butter
3 oz (75 g) brown sugar
4 oz (100 g) sultanas
4 oz (100 g) currants
2 oz (50 g) raisins
1 teaspoon of ground ginger
1 teaspoon of cinnamon
Half a teaspoon of mixed spice
Quarter-teaspoon of salt
2 tablespoons of treacle or syrup
2 eggs
Milk to mix

- Set a large pot half-filled with water, to boil. As it does, drop in a clean white lint-free cotton or linen cloth to boil for some minutes before fishing it out with tongs and leaving it to steam. When you can without scalding your hands, peel it apart to spread it out, and dust it liberally with flour.
- Mix all the dry ingredients together.
- Dissolve the treacle or syrup in the milk and eggs and add this to the dry ingredients to make a soft, dripping consistency.
- Put it into the cloth and tie it up, leaving some room for the dumpling to expand.
- Slip a saucer or plate into the bottom of the pot, and put the dumpling on it.

- Add more boiling water to come almost to the top of the dumpling, cover and let it steam for 3–4 hours.
- Alternatively, the dumpling can be cooked in a bowl in the way of a normal steamed pudding, but it will not have the skin that being boiled in a floured cloth gives it.
- After it has cooked, plunge the dumpling into a basin of cold water for 10 seconds, then remove it to an oven-proof dish to dry off for a few minutes in a moderate oven.
- It can be left as it is, or sprinkled with caster sugar.
- Eat it as a pudding or in slices, fried, with a hearty bacon and sausage breakfast.

Whisky Toddy Cake

*T he sweet lemon and whisky flavours of this cake and its
lemon drizzle icing are deliciously reminiscent of the
same warming flavours in a hot whisky toddy.*

Cake
Grated rind of a lemon (use the juice for the icing)
8 oz (225 g) sultanas
5 fl oz (140 ml) of whisky
6 oz (175 g) butter, softened
6 oz (175 g) soft brown sugar
3 eggs, separated
6 oz (175 g) plain flour
1 teaspoon of baking powder
Icing
Juice of a lemon
8 oz (225 g) icing sugar
A little warm water

Oven temperature: 180 °C, 350 °F, Gas Mark 4

- Put the lemon rind and sultanas in a bowl and pour the
  whisky over them; leave overnight to soak.
- The next day, cream the butter and sugar together until
  they are light and fluffy.
- To this mixture, beat in the egg yolks one by one,
  adding a teaspoonful of sifted flour with each to stop
  the mixture curdling; beat well after each addition.
- Then fold in fruit and whisky mixture.
- Sift the flour and baking powder together; fold them
  in.
- Finally, whisk the egg whites until they are stiff and
  fold them into the cake mixture.
- Turn the mix out into a pre-greased cake tin lined with
  baking parchment.

- Bake the cake in the pre-heated oven for around one-and-a-half hours, or until a skewer inserted into the centre comes out dry. Remove from the oven and cool on a wire rack.
- While the cake is cooling, make the icing by mixing the lemon juice into the sieved icing sugar together with, added a little at a time, enough warm water to give the icing a pouring consistency.
- Spoon the icing over the cake to let it drizzle over the top and down the sides.

Dundee Cake

6 oz (175 g) butter
6 oz (175 g) sugar
4 eggs
1 oz (25 g) ground almonds
Grated rind of an orange
Grated rind of a lemon
8 oz (225g) plain flour
6 oz (175 g) sultanas
6 oz (175 g) currants
6 oz (175 g) raisins
4 oz (100 g) chopped mixed peel
3 tablespoons of orange liqueur such as Glayva or Aurum
4 oz (100 g) blanched whole almonds

Oven temperature: 325 °F, 170 °C, Gas Mark 3

- Two days before you make the cake, put the dried fruits and mixed peel into a bowl with the liqueur and give it all a good stir; mix it up again occasionally.
- Cream the butter and the sugar together until light and fluffy. Whisk the eggs individually and add each with a teaspoonful of sifted flour to the creamed mixture; beat well after each one.
- Stir in the ground almonds, the fruit rinds and the dried fruit-and-spirit mixture. Finally, sieve the flour and baking powder over the mixture and fold it in. The mixture should be soft enough to drop off a spoon, so if it is too stiff, add a tiny splash of milk.
- Turn the mixture out into an 8 inch (20 cm) pre-greased cake tin. Smooth it level and sit the almonds in concentric circles on top, taking care not to push them in too much.
- Bake in the pre-heated oven for around 2 hours, or until a skewer inserted into the centre comes out dry.
- Remove from the oven and leave to cool.

Tablet

*M*ore brittle than fudge but softer than toffee, tablet is a sweet-lover's dream but is also a dental disaster and, consequently, a special-occasion treat.

7 oz (200 g) tin condensed milk
1 lb (450 g) granulated sugar
5 oz (150 g) butter
4 fl oz (110 ml) of milk

- In a heavy-based pan, melt the butter.
- Add the milk, sugar and condensed milk and simmer on a low heat for about 20 minutes or until the mixture reaches 115 °C/240 °F on a sugar thermometer. If you do not have a sugar thermometer, watch for the mixture coming away from the side of the pan as it simmers, then use this test: drop some of the mixture into a cup of cold water and leave for some moments before picking it up; you should be able to roll it into a soft ball between your fingers.
- Take the pan off the heat and beat the mixture well, with a wooden spoon, scraping in all the solidifying tablet from the edges, for 5 minutes; when it is no longer thin, but not so solid that it cannot pour, turn it out into shallow, lightly greased tins and mark the mixture off into squares as it cools.

- Flavourings can be mixed into the tablet after you take it off the heat.

Vanilla: Beat in 3 drops of vanilla essence.
Fruit and Nut: Beat in 2 oz (50 g) raisins and 2 oz (50 g) nuts.
Cinnamon: Beat in 3 scant teaspoons of ground cinnamon.
Chocolate: Beat in 3 scant teaspoons of cocoa powder.
Mint: Beat in 3 drops of peppermint oil.

Butterscotch

1 lb (450 g) brown sugar
4 fl oz (110 ml) of milk
4 oz (100 g) butter
1 level teaspoon of ground ginger or 2 teaspoons of lemon juice

- Put the sugar and milk in a heavy pan and bring to the boil, stirring all the time to make sure that the sugar dissolves.
- Beat the butter, either in a food mixer or with a wooden spoon, until creamed, then add this to the melted-sugar mixture, stir it in and bring all to the boil again.
- Simmer the mixture, stirring continuously, on a low heat for about 25 minutes or until it reaches 121 °C/250 °F on a sugar thermometer. If you do not have a sugar thermometer, watch for the mixture coming away from the side of the pan as it simmers, then use this test: drop some of the mixture into a cup of cold water and leave for some moments before picking it up; the mixture should form a hard ball in the water.
- Take the pan off the heat and beat in your chosen flavouring of ginger or lemon.
- Beat the mixture well, with a wooden spoon, scraping in all the solidifying butterscotch from the edges, for 5 minutes; when it is no longer thin, but not so solid that it cannot pour, turn it out into shallow, lightly buttered tins and mark the mixture off into squares as it cools.
- When it has cooled completely, turn it upside down to get it out then tap it on the back with a heavy instrument – a toffee hammer, heavy knife handle or large pair of scissors will do – to break it into squares.
- Keep it in a polythene bag or airtight container.

Blairgowrie
Raspberry Vinegar

This is a good and unusual way of using up overripe soft fruit, and strawberries, loganberries, blackberries and blackcurrants can be substituted for raspberries as the main flavouring.

1 lb (450 g) raspberries
1 pint (570 ml) of white wine or cider vinegar
Sugar to taste (see recipe)

- Sort out the fruit, discarding any stale berries, leaves or stalks.
- Crush it with a wooden masher or the back of a wooden spoon and pour the vinegar over it.
- Cover the bowl and leave it for 3 or 4 days, stirring the mixture once or twice a day.
- Then, to strain off the juice, tip everything into a jelly bag (a nylon sieve lined with gauze will also do) and leave it overnight to drip.
- The next day measure the juice and put it in a pan, adding anything from no sugar up to 14 oz (400 g) of sugar per pint (570 ml) for every pint of juice, to get the vinegar to your preferred taste.
- If you do add the sugar, stir the mixture over a low heat to make sure it dissolves.
- Bring it to the boil, then let it simmer for 10 minutes.
- Bottle it in pre-washed sterilised bottles (see p.57 for sterilising instructions).

Dundee Marmalade

*M*armalade's unusual name is explained in a story which also dates its first appearance in Scotland. When the newly widowed Queen Mary was returning home to Scotland in 1561 after the death of her husband, the king of France, she was said to have brought an orange preserve on board to counteract her seasickness. When a Scottish courtier asked what it was, the queen replied, 'C'est pour ma malade'. But as is so often the case, this pretty story is, sadly, almost certainly untrue. Marmalade was first made commercially in Scotland by the Keiller family of Dundee, where they opened the country's first marmalade factory in 1797.

Makes about 5–6 lb.

2 lb (910 g) Seville oranges
2 lemons
4 pints (2.25 l) of water
4 lb (1.8 kg) granulated, preserving or brown sugar

- Scrub the oranges and lemons and add them whole to the water in a heavy-based, deep-sided pan.
- Cover, bring to the boil then lower the heat to simmer for around one-and-a-half to two hours, until the skins are soft and can be pricked easily.
- Lift the fruits out, let them cool, then quarter them.
- Take out the pips and return these to the liquid in the pan, to boil for 10 minutes.
- Meanwhile, slice up the fruit to the thickness you prefer; Dundee marmalade traditionally has quite a coarse cut.
- Strain the liquid to remove the pips again, then put the sliced fruit back into the liquid.
- Bring to the boil then add the sugar. When it has melted, boil again, rapidly and without stirring, until the mixture gets to setting point (104 or 105 °C or

220 °F on a sugar thermometer); this can take 15–30 minutes.

- Turn down the heat while you test the marmalade. If you have no thermometer, drop a teaspoonful onto a chilled saucer; if it solidifies and forms a skin, it will set.
- Take the pan off, scrape off any scum and let the marmalade sit in the pan for 15 minutes to set and cool.
- Stir it before potting in pre-washed and still-warm sterilised* jars, and cover immediately.

- For a special marmalade with a particularly Scottish kick, stir in some whisky. Use a good blend like Black Bottle, or one of the mellower or sweeter malts, if you can spare any. Fill a 1 lb jar of marmalade not quite full, leaving enough space to stir in a tablespoon of spirit at the top. Drambuie and Glayva will also both complement and sweeten the tartness of Dundee marmalade very nicely.

* To sterilise the jars, wash them in soapy water, dry them thoroughly then pop them in an oven at 180 °C, 350 °F, Gas Mark 4 for 5 minutes. As a rule, you should avoid potting hot preserves into cold jars.

Wild Bramble Jelly

Scotland's mild, temperate summers are well suited for berry-growing in the country's drier regions, but soft fruits like raspberries, blaeberries and brambles can also be found growing wild, not just on country walks but also in city backcourts and lanes.

Makes about 3 lb.

2 lb (910 g) brambles
10 fl oz (280 ml) of water
Juice of 1 lemon
Sugar (see recipe for amount)

- ❧ Put the brambles, water and lemon juice into a deep-sided pan and cook gently for about 30 minutes or until the fruit is softened.
- ❧ Leave in the pan to cool, then strain through a jelly bag (a nylon sieve lined with gauze will also do) and leave it overnight to drip.
- ❧ Measure the water back into the cleaned pan, adding 1 lb (450 g) of sugar for every pint (570 ml) of liquid.
- ❧ Heat it gently, stirring until the sugar has dissolved.
- ❧ Then bring it up to a rapid boil, and carry on boiling the mixture until it reaches the setting point (104 or 105 °C or 220 °F on a sugar thermometer).
- ❧ Turn down the heat while you test the jelly. If you have no thermometer, drop a teaspoonful onto a chilled saucer; if it solidifies and forms a skin, it will set.
- ❧ Pot it in pre-washed and still-warm sterilised jars (see p.57 for sterilising instructions), and cover immediately.

Rowan Jelly

The tartness of traditional rowan jelly makes it the ideal accompaniment for game dishes, such as roast venison, pheasant or grouse.

Makes about 4–5 lb.

> 2 lb (910 g) rowan (mountain ash) berries
> 2 lb (910 g) cooking apples, chopped
> Water
> Sugar (see recipe for amount)

NB: For a more astringent jelly, vary the proportions of the main ingredients to 3 lb (1.4 kg) berries and 1 lb (450 g) fruit.

- ⍥ Rinse and drain the rowan berries and pull them off their stalks.
- ⍥ Put them in a deep-sided pan, then add the chopped apples and enough water to cover both.
- ⍥ Bring the mixture up to the boil, then simmer for 45 minutes or until the berries are soft.
- ⍥ To strain off the juice, tip everything into a jelly bag (a nylon sieve lined with gauze will also do) and leave it overnight to drip.
- ⍥ The next day measure the juice and put it in a pan, adding 1 lb (450g) of sugar for every pint (570 ml) of juice.
- ⍥ Bring to the boil, stirring to make sure the sugar is completely dissolved, then simmer until the mixture gets to setting point (104 or 105 °C or 220 °F on a sugar thermometer).
- ⍥ Turn down the heat while you test the jelly. If you have no thermometer, drop a teaspoonful onto a chilled saucer; if it solidifies and forms a skin, it will set.
- ⍥ Pot it in pre-washed and still-warm sterilised jars (see p.57 for sterilising instructions), and cover immediately.

Porridge

*M*uch that can be described as at best mythology and at worst nonsense about the Scots and their attitude to porridge is still written by food writers and book editors who should know better. These assertions are generally of the 'Scots still eat their porridge well salted' and 'Scots are contemptuous of those who add sugar to porridge' variety.

⊗ Unfortunately for such culinary romantics, speed rather than anything else determines the content of most Scots break-fasts, and early-morning arguments are more likely to revolve around where the cornflakes packet can be, rather than on types of porridge flavouring. And, with a complete disregard for alleged national attributes, Scots are just as likely as any-one else to eat their oats in muesli-form rather than porridge.

⊗ But for all those, Scots and outlanders, who wish a hearty, healthy, cheap and sustaining (albeit time-consuming) breakfast, this is the way to make porridge.

Serves 2.

1 pint (570 ml) of water
2.5 oz (70 g) medium oatmeal
A scant teaspoon of salt

⊗ Put the water in a pot and bring it up to a rolling boil.

⊗ Pour the oatmeal in gradually but continuously, all the time stirring to make sure it does not go lumpy. When the mixture returns to the boil, cover it and turn it down to simmer gently for 15 minutes.

⊗ Stir in the salt, cover again and let it cook for 10 minutes or so, depending on how thick you prefer it.

⊗ Serve the porridge either on its own or with a sprinkling of sugar on top, with a separate bowl of milk, cream or yoghurt (each individual spoonful is then dipped into it, so it does not cool the surface of the porridge) or with honey or syrup.

Whisky Toddy

A nother winter warmer, this time in liquid form. This traditional Scottish tonic for the common cold may not be as effective as Lem Sip at treating your symptoms, but it will make you forget about them a lot quicker.

5 fl oz (140 ml) of boiling water
1 measure of whisky, heated
Juice of half a lemon, heated
1 teaspoon of honey, preferably heather honey

- Put a metal spoon into a glass (this prevents the glass cracking with the hot water) and pour in the whisky, lemon juice and boiling water and stir.
- Spoon in the honey and stir again until it dissolves.
- Taste it, and make appropriate adjustments to the ingredients according to personal preference.

Notes for North American Cooks

Dry ingredients

The British cooking system generally measures by weight, the American by volume. The following are some common ingredients by weight and their approximate American equivalents.

- 4 oz flour = 1 cup
  4 oz medium, coarse or pinhead oatmeal = 1 cup
  3 oz rice = 1 cup (scant)
  2 oz fresh breadcrumbs = 1 cup

- 4 oz butter = 1 stick
  1 oz butter = 2 tablespoons
  4 oz double (heavy) cream = 1 cup
  8 oz curd cheese = 1 cup
  5 oz soft cheese = two-thirds of a cup
  4 oz Cheddar cheese, grated = 1 cup

- 7 oz lard = 1 cup
  4 oz shredded suet = 1 cup

- 7 oz cooked mashed potatoes = 1 cup

- 6 oz sultanas = 1 cup

- 8 oz granulated or caster sugar = 1 cup
  4 oz icing sugar (confectioner's sugar) = 1 cup

Liquids

There are also differences in liquid measurements, a British (Imperial) pint being 20 fl oz, and an American being 16 fl oz. So for British recipes which call for quarter of a pint, American cooks should use 5 fl oz, and 10 fl oz where the recipe calls for half a pint.

Scottish Food by Mail Order

Please note: This list is not exhaustive.

Smoked Fish & Products
Alba Smokehouse, Kilmory, Lochgilphead,
Argyll PA31 8RR
Tel: 01546-604400
Fax: 01546-604400

Cheeses
Iain J. Mellis, Cheesemonger, 205 Bruntsfield Place,
Edinburgh EH10 4DH
Tel: 0131-447 8889
Fax: 0131-447 7001

Meat & Poultry
Organic Meat & Products (Scotland)
Jamesfield Farm, By Newburgh, Fife KY14 6EW
Tel: 01738-850498
Fax: 01738-850741

Venison
Fletchers of Auchtermuchty, Reediehill Deer Farm,
Auchtermuchty, Fife KY14 7HS
Tel: 01337-828369
Fax: 01337-827001
Website: http://www.gourmetworld.co.uk:80/fletchers/index.html

Haggis
MacSween of Edinburgh, Dryden Road, Bilston Glen, Loanhead,
Edinburgh EH20 9LZ
Tel: 0131-440 2555
Fax: 0131-440 2674

Whiskies, Liqueurs & Spirits
Loch Fyne Whiskies, Inveraray, Argyll PA32 8UD
Tel: 01499-302219
Fax: 01499-302238

COLLINS

Other titles in *The Scottish Collection* series are:

Scottish Verse
ISBN 0 00 472166 7
£4.99

Homelands of the Clans
ISBN 0 00 472165 9
£4.99

Classic Malts
ISBN 0 00 472068 7
£4.99